D0177481

C152829036

No Limits

SKATEBOARDING

Jed Morgan

W
FRANKLIN WATTS
LONDON • SYDNEY

First published in 2005 by
Franklin Watts
96 Leonard Street
London
EC2A 4XD

Franklin Watts Australia
45–51 Huntley Street
Alexandria, NSW 2015

Series editor: Adrian Cole
Series design: Pewter Design Associates
Art director: Jonathan Hair
Picture researcher: Sophie Hartley

A CIP catalogue record for this book is available from the British Library.

ISBN: 0 7496 5823 1

Printed in Malaysia

The author and publisher would like to thank the following people
for their contribution to the production of this book:
Darren Rathbone at Shiner (www.shiner.co.uk), Patty Segovia – All Girl Skate Jam
(www.allgirlskatejam.com), Last Resort Picture Library (dmimaging.co.uk), Lush
Longboards (www.lushlongboards.com) and Darryl Franklin at www.dannyway.com

Acknowledgements:
The Publisher acknowledges all © products shown within
this title as the property of their respective owners.

Tony Donaldson/Action Plus: 29t. Tim Leighton-Boyce/Action
Plus: Cover. © Bettmann/Corbis: 4. © Strauss/Curtis/Corbis:
14t. © John-Marshall Mantel/Corbis: 13tr. © Mike
McGill/Corbis: 14b, 21b. © Al Fuchs/NewSport/Corbis: 17r,
21tr, 26b, 28t. © Matthew Kasperek/NewSport/Corbis: 8t.
© Rick Rickman/NewSport/Corbis: 10. © Eric Perlman/Corbis:
9b. © Phil Schermeister/Corbis: 5tl. © Ted Soqui/Corbis: 23b.
© Paul A. Souders/Corbis: 15. © Michael S. Yamashita/Corbis:
26t. © Jess Dyrenforth: 8b, 18, 19t, 24, 27b. Kim Myung Jung
Kim/PA/Empics: 28b. Last Resort Picture Library: 12, 13cl, 20,
22t & b, 23t. courtesy Lush Longboards Ltd: 9t. ©Styley/
PYMCA: 25t. David Thorpe/Rex Features: 5tr. Courtesy Shiner
Ltd. www.shiner.co.uk: 5b, 6-7 all, 11 all, 13tl, bl & br, 25b.
© Patty Segovia/Silver Photo Agency: 16, 21tl, 29b.
courtesy DannyWay.com, Photo by Blabac. © DC Shoes Inc.:
17l, 27t. Courtesy DannyWay.com, © 2004 Tony Vu/
Shazaam/ESPN Images: 19b.

Whilst every attempt has been made to clear copyright
should there be any inadvertent omission please apply
in the first instance to the publisher regarding rectification.

To follow the skateboard
industry standard, all
skateboard measurements in
this book are in inches.
All other measurements are
in centimetres and metres.

Impotant Note:

Disclaimer – In the preparation of this
book all due care has been exercised with
regard to the activities depicted. The
Publishers regret that they can accept no
liability for any loss or injury sustained.

Contents

World of skateboarding

Whether you want to jam in the local skatepark or just muck about with friends, skateboarding is a great way to get around in today's busy world.

To the limit

The early skateboards had clay wheels that had little grip. Several accidents (including some deaths) and a public outcry about dangerous skateboarders led to a decline in the sport after 1965.

Skateboarding is born

As far back as the early 1900s, people were experimenting with early skateboards by fixing roller skate wheels to pieces of wood. The big break for skateboards came in the early 1960s when Larry Stevenson began to promote the skateboard for 'surfing the streets' in the USA. In 1963, his company 'Mahaka' made the first professional skateboards. Within just a few years, over 50 million skateboards had been sold.

Four boys surf the streets on their skateboards in Chicago, USA, 1965.

Plastic Fantastic

Frank Nasworthy introduced new plastic (polyurethane) wheels in 1973 that gave skateboards much greater control. The new wheels led to a skateboard boom and by 1976 the sport had its own magazines, and its first purpose-built skateboard park in Florida, USA. By 1980, the craze for new BMX bikes saw skateboarding decline in popularity again. But hardcore boarders kept the sport alive and today it is more popular than ever.

Ready on the ramp, 1980s. Skateboard fashion has changed over the years.

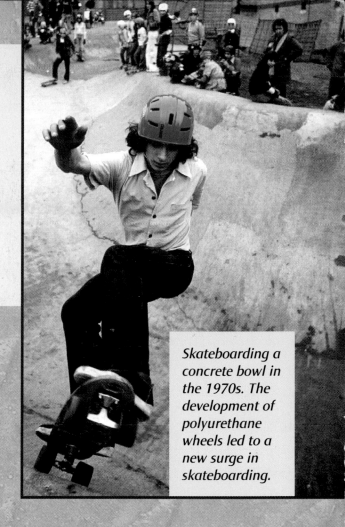

Skateboarding a concrete bowl in the 1970s. The development of polyurethane wheels led to a new surge in skateboarding.

FROM THE EDGE

'Skateboarding has not yet reached its maximum potential, and who can say what the limits are? To find out grab that board! You don't have to be a super-talented professional skater – grab that board if you're a novice just having some fun on a Saturday afternoon.' Extract from the first edition of *Thrasher* skateboard magazine, 1981

The skateboard craze

As well as magazines there are now skateboarding films, websites and even computer games, as well as thousands of skateboard shops. The sport now has worldwide competitions including its own showcase, the X-Games. It is a billion pound industry with top pros earning thousands of pounds in prize and sponsorship money.

Thrasher magazine today. Many skateboard magazines have helped to promote the sport.

Know your skateboard

Today, skateboards use the latest materials and technology to provide the ultimate ride. This Bullet 'Bird' shares four basic elements with all skateboards — the deck, trucks, wheels and bearings.

DECK

✴ Normally made of 7 layers (plies) of maple wood that are glued (laminated) together and shaped under high-pressure.

✴ Decks can be up to 9-ply, which makes them stronger, but also heavier.

✴ Deck width — a good all-round deck is 8 inches wide — this is what most beginners will learn on. Wider decks of 8–8.5 inches are preferred by vert or ramp skaters, while street and trick skaters use narrower decks of 7.5–7.75 inches.

GRIP TAPE

The top of the deck has a gritty covering called grip tape that helps your feet grip the board.

Deck base – normally printed with eye-catching graphics and the manufacturer's logo.

SHOCK PADS

These rubber pads fit between the base of the deck and the top of the trucks. They help reduce shocks for a smoother ride.

King pin

Axle

Base plate

Bushing

TRUCKS

* They bolt to the base of your deck and hold the wheels.
* They are made up of several parts, but are normally sold as a unit.
* The axle length of trucks varies, but should not stick out beyond the rail of your deck (unless you have a longboard – see page 9).
* Long axles make the board turn more slowly.
* Short axles make the board turn quickly.
* Trucks have an adjustable plastic bushing that works a bit like a shock absorber and controls the feel of the board. The tighter you make the bush the harder (less spongy) your turns will feel.

HOT HINT

Complete or custom-built? It is easy to build your own skateboard by buying the parts separately. This is well worth it as you get into skateboarding. A custom board can be expensive though, so if you're just starting out buy a complete board. This will be good enough to learn on and give you time to plan and save up for your perfect board!

Wheel – 54mm
Bullet-proof
polyurethane
Bearings – ABEC3

Truck – 125mm, non-slip axle, high-grade aluminium

WHEELS

Wheels are made from polyurethane compound (a type of plastic) and vary in size and hardness.
* Sizes range from 49mm to 72mm in diameter.
* Large wheels increase speed and stability.
* Small wheels (49–58mm) are better for tricks and street skating.
* Hardness is measured in durometers from 99 (the softest) to 101 (the hardest). Hard wheels are faster and last longer, but soft wheels give a smoother ride.

Cool science

Bearings fit inside the wheel and allow it to spin freely around the axle. There are many types and most, but not all, are rated with a number (normally 1, 3, 5 or 7). The higher the number the faster the bearing will turn. Bearings are a standard size and will fit any wheel.

A skateboard for all

Choosing the right skateboard depends on what you want to do with it. Skateboard shop staff will help you to consider all the options, but here is the lowdown on some of the main board types.

HOT HINT

Remember that most skateboarding components will fit any deck. Try swapping parts with friends and see what board set up best suits you.

Vert boards

If you want to spend most of your time at the local skatepark and perfect those vert ramps, then these are the boards for you. A vert board is normally wider than a standard board with 8.25 or 8.5 inch decks being the most common. Larger and softer wheels are normally chosen by vert riders as they give greater stability for riding the ramps.

Vert boards, such as this one, are wider to give greater stability on ramps.

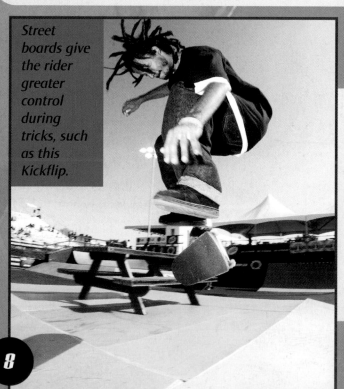

Street boards give the rider greater control during tricks, such as this Kickflip.

Street/Technical boards

If you're going to be skating in your own neighbourhood or around town then you'll need one of these boards. Street or technical skating (see page 19) involves lots of grinds, flip tricks and other technical moves. Street boards have a narrower deck of around 7.5 – 8.0 inches and smaller, harder wheels to make it easier to flip the board or perform jumps.

Cruisers

If you will mainly use your skateboard for cruising then it's best to get a longer deck. This will give you greater balance and control. Larger and softer wheels will increase your speed and help you ride out bumps and cracks in the pavement. For serious cruising you may want to choose a longboard.

Longboards

These are longer skateboards that range in length from around 36 inches to a whopping 60 inches! The decks are often shaped with a more pointed nose and tail than other decks and are also wider in the middle (9 inches or more). The trucks and wheels on many longboards stick out beyond the edge of the deck. This gives greater manoeuvrability and prevents the wheels catching the board when carving (turning) at high speeds. Longboards are the speed freaks' dream and great for cruising.

Lush longboard 'Legend'.

FROM THE EDGE

'Longboards, with their smooth-turning trucks, and fast wheels, give a flowing, carving ride that can be everything from chilled-out cruising to extreme high-speed slides, depending on your mood. The Legend has a 48 inch deck, and features Lush L125 trucks, Kryptonics 65mm wheels and Lush Swiss ABEC5 bearings'.
Lush website www.lushlongboards.com

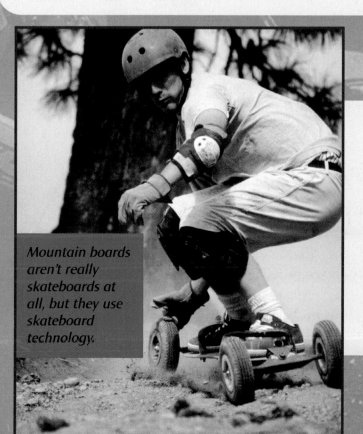

Mountain boards aren't really skateboards at all, but they use skateboard technology.

Mountain boards

Mountain boards use skateboard technology, but have adapted it for off-road boarding by adding specialist trucks and air-filled tyres. The boards are long and use materials such as fibreglass, carbon fibre and wood. This is to keep them strong but lightweight. Mountain boards also have a binding system similar to that on a snowboard. This straps your feet to the board and improves your board control.

Get geared up

There is more skateboard gear than there are skateboards, but it is not just about looking good. Skateboard gear is designed to let you skate to your limits, and stay in one piece at the same time.

Skate shoes

You can skate in any shoe, but skate shoes will dramatically improve your comfort and performance. They are made of soft materials to let your foot flex, and have wide, flat soles with sticky rubber to help you stay on the deck. Skate shoes have become popular general street fashion in recent years, so there are now hundreds to choose from. Your local skate store will help you select the right ones for you.

Patches

These are a great way to customise your clothing to fit your own image. They are produced by a wide range of manufacturers and are available from all good skateboard shops.

Many skateboarders wear skate-style shoes. The wide soles greatly enhance rider performance.

Clothes

There are no rules with skateboard clothing. Some skaters prefer shorts, others long trousers. Some like hooded tops, known as 'hoodies', while others choose shirts or T-shirts. The important thing is that you feel comfortable. For most skaters a pair of loose-fitting jeans (to allow movement) and a cotton T-shirt are ideal.

HOT HINT

If you can't find a T-shirt or hoodie you like, why not design your own and have it printed? This doesn't cost much and makes you stand out from the crowd. Many skateboard pros have developed their own designs like this.

Helmet

Concussion and similar head injuries can be avoided if you wear a helmet. There are so many to choose from, there's not really an excuse for not having one. They are lightweight and fully ventilated, so won't affect your skateboarding performance. Ask the staff at your local skate shop to make sure your helmet is a good fit. An incorrectly-fitted helmet is almost as bad as not having one at all. If you take any serious hits then get it checked out and replace it if necessary.

Pads and guards

Even if you think a grazed elbow looks cool, knee and elbow pads provide vital protection. These are the parts most likely to scrape along the ground when you fall. Knee pads are particularly important in vert skating, so that you can slide down the ramp on them when you fail to land a trick. Some pads can be worn under your clothing. Wrist guards are gloves with a rib of metal or toughened plastic inside. They should be worn whatever your skate style.

Get ready to go

The best riders work as one with their boards. They provide the energy, steering and lift that are needed to make the board perform to its limit. Your body will do a lot of the work, so it's important to get it ready for action.

A good stretch

Stretches are a way of preparing your muscles for work. Move slowly into each stretch and hold it for about 15 seconds. Repeat each stretch several times on each side of your body. Hip and hamstring stretches are the most useful for skateboarding

A hamstring stretch helps a rider to warm up his muscles.

Hips

Stand with your feet slightly apart and your arms stretched out ahead. Keeping your lower body still, rotate slowly from the waist to one side and then the other. Next, put your hands on your hips and lean over to the side. Do this several times and repeat for the other side. Keeping your hands on your hips, gently rotate your hips in a circle.

Hamstring

Stand with your legs apart and put both hands together. Bend at the waist and try to touch the ground between your legs. Repeat several times, but come up each time — don't bounce! Now try to touch each toe by reaching to the side as you bend. Repeat several times for each side.

Board Fit

Always check out your board before you head out (see below right). It won't need much maintenance, but eventually parts will wear out and they'll need to be replaced. Always keep spare parts handy so you can get skating straightaway. These parts include rubber bushings and metal retainer cups (1), truck bolts (2) and axle nuts (3).

A board sustains damage when you perform tricks. Remember to check your one before riding it.

Customise your board

Customising your board is the easiest thing in the world and can be done cheaply by using manufacturers' stickers (right). Next time you come to replace your wheels, check out the full range. Wheels are a distinctive way to make your board stand out. You could even update your trucks to bring new life to your old board.

HOT HINT

Before you head out:

1. DECK — Never ride a board if you think it is damaged – ask staff at your local skate shop to check it out if you're not sure ✔

2. GRIP TAPE — Make sure the grip tape on the deck is clean. Brush off any excess dirt ✔

3. WHEELS — Make sure they are not worn, replace them if big chunks of 'urethane are missing. Make sure the wheels spin freely – service or replace noisy bearings ✔

4. TRUCKS — Check the mounting hardware (truck bolts, etc) to make sure it's tight ✔

5. AXLE NUTS — Make sure these are secure; suddenly skating on three wheels isn't fun ✔

POWELL

Play it safe

Skateboarding is all about having fun and pushing yourself to the extremes, but it can be dangerous to yourself and others. By following some simple guidelines and playing it safe you can avoid most problems.

Look after yourself

All the padding in the world will not protect you if you try to out trick yourself. Don't be in a rush to perfect your skating style. It is far better to take things slowly and master each level of skill as you go. If you can, try out new moves over a soft surface, such as grass as this will help cushion your fall. Don't be afraid to ask for advice from more experienced skaters.

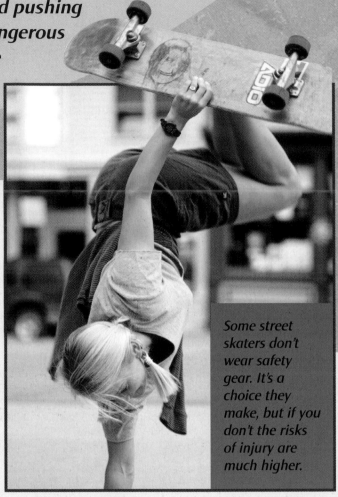

Some street skaters don't wear safety gear. It's a choice they make, but if you don't the risks of injury are much higher.

HOT HINT

'Don't skate mad — think about what you're doing all the time. Use your head, that's the best piece of safety advice I can give — stay alert, stay alive.'
Bethany Green, skateboard instructor

Look out for others

You will often find yourself practising tricks and skating in public places. In recent years, some skateboarders have given the sport a bad name by ignoring the safety of others. Thankfully, today most skateboarders behave responsibly. Remember to share spaces with other skaters and always give way to pedestrians. The elderly, very young and animals can find a fast approaching skateboard especially frightening.

Respect the rules

Skateboarding has been banned from some busy public areas, but there are special parks you can use. If you don't know where these are, then ask your local council for information. Many skaters are pushing for special skate zones, but these will only be granted if skaters respect the rules that already exist. You should always be careful not to trespass onto private property even if it has irresistible steps, rails and walls for jumps and grinds.

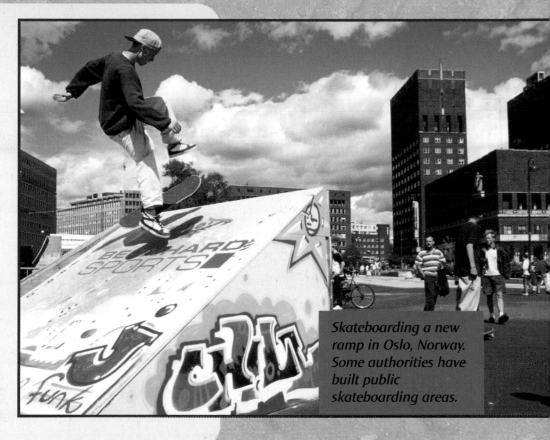

Skateboarding a new ramp in Oslo, Norway. Some authorities have built public skateboarding areas.

FROM THE EDGE

'Cities and municipalities have an obligation to their communities to provide safe places for their youth to skate. It is an investment in their future.'
Skate Park Association of the United States of America (SPAUSA)

Skate smart

Safety tips for skateboarders:
* Make sure all equipment is in good condition and fits properly.
* Always wear a helmet, and replace it every 2–3 years or after a major impact.
* Wrist guards will help to prevent wrist fractures in case of falls.
* Choose a safe location, away from traffic.
* Learn how to control speed and stop.
* Do not wear headphones.
* Do not skate at night or in wet conditions.
* STAY ALERT! Keep your eyes on the surface ahead; watch for other people, cars and hazards such as cracks, rocks, etc.
* Respect others around you.

Just For Fun

Skateboarding may well be a billion pound international sport, but most skaters do it just for the fun. For millions, skateboarding is simply a way to get together with board buddies.

Hire or borrow

If you are tempted by skateboarding, but don't want to splash out on your own board just yet, then why not try hiring or borrowing one. Find out if your local skatepark has a hire scheme. Better still, see if you can borrow one from a more experienced skater. There is a good chance they will have more than one. By hiring or borrowing you can check out the sport before spending your cash. Be warned though, skateboarding is the only thing you'll want to do once you've tried it!

Free Fun

The best thing about skateboarding is that once you have a basic board and safety gear it is a virtually free sport. You can wear whatever you want and skate wherever you are allowed to. The only costs will be your maintenance costs and those tempting upgrades.

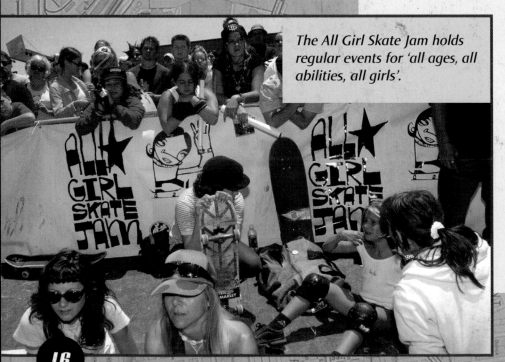

The All Girl Skate Jam holds regular events for 'all ages, all abilities, all girls'.

Skate clubs

Take your skateboard experience to another level by joining a skateboard club in your area. Many of them arrange regular jams and may even have their own vert ramps. A club can also be a great place to pick up tricks and tips, and of course to meet new skaters. If there is no club in your area, why not get together with your buddies and start your own.

FROM THE EDGE

'Just go out there and have fun and do what you normally do. If you go out there and your main purpose is to get a sponsor, then it's not gonna work. Just go out there and have fun. That's how I got sponsored.' Ryan Sheckler (right), pro skateboarder and X-Games gold medalist

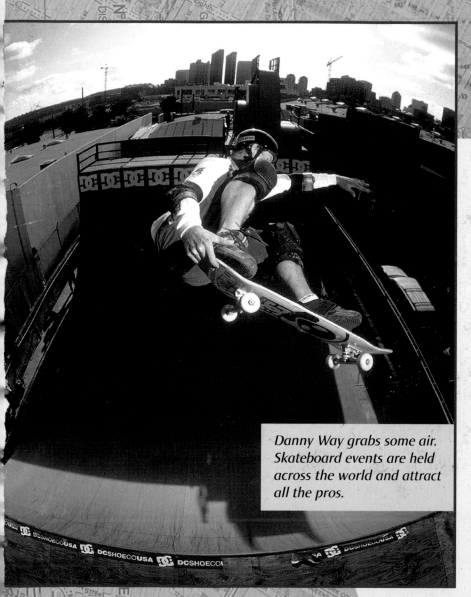

Danny Way grabs some air. Skateboard events are held across the world and attract all the pros.

Skateboard events

There is nothing to beat the thrill of watching real skateboard pros in action. You will be amazed at how high they can jump and how fast they can travel. The best chance to see them is at one of the regional, national or international competitions, but these might be too far away for you to get to. Another good way to catch them is to keep an eye out for special events in your area. Skateboarding manufacturers often put together showcase events. They invite pros who show off the products in action. Your local skate shop or club will probably know of upcoming events, so go along and be inspired.

Skateboarding sports

Skateboarding can be divided into several different sports, each with its own specialist skills. All of them test speed, strength, timing and nerves.

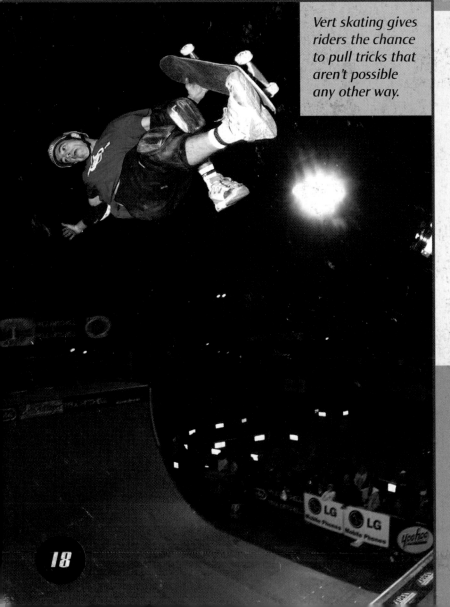

Vert skating gives riders the chance to pull tricks that aren't possible any other way.

Vert skating

If you like the look of seriously big air then Vert skating is the sport for you. Vert (meaning vertical) skaters use halfpipes to build up speed and pull tricks before trying to land back on the ramp. Most skateparks will have at least one vert ramp and maybe several of differing sizes. A normal ramp is around 3.5m high and about 9m wide, but they vary greatly and each has its own challenges. In recent years, top skaters have pushed beyond the vert ramp to the super ramp (6m high) and now even the mega ramp with a halfpipe over 8m high!

To the limit

Using the mega ramp that he invented, Danny Way holds the World Record for the longest skateboard jump of 24 metres and the biggest air of over 7 metres.

Street skating

This is the most popular form of skateboarding today because you can do it almost anywhere. The kerbs, walls, steps and rails that are found in any town or city are all challenging obstacles to the street skater. The streets outside the South Bank arts centre in London have been a favourite hang out for street skaters since the 1970s. Many people have complained about skaters damaging the area, but in 2004 a series of five 'skateable' sculptures were introduced and skateboarding was officially welcomed on the South Bank. Not everywhere is as welcoming to street skaters though. Make sure you check out where is hot and where not to skate.

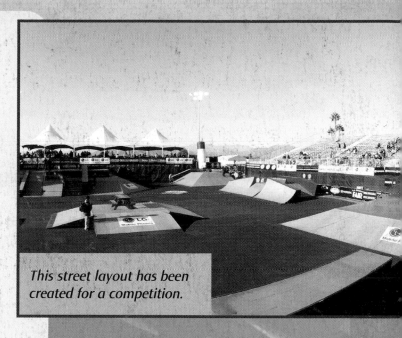

This street layout has been created for a competition.

FROM THE EDGE

'I didn't plan on breaking any records, I'm just stoked to see skateboarding progress and go to a higher level...' Danny Way (below) after breaking the longest air World Record at the X-Games in August 2004

Slalom skateboarding

This is one of the oldest types of skateboarding and was popular in the 1960s and 1970s. Riders have to pass down a course through a number of gates (normally cones) in the fastest time possible. Most races are against the clock with the fastest rider winning. Slalom skateboarding began a comeback in 2001 with the first World Championships for nearly 20 years. Its popularity has also been helped by the new longboards — perfect for fast turns. There are now regular races across the USA and Europe.

Getting started

Once you have your board you will be desperate to pull those big air tricks, but it is important to master the basics first. They will make you a better rider and stop you picking up injuries, too.

Get the stance

You stand sideways on a skateboard with your feet spaced about shoulder width apart. Keep your knees slightly bent and use your arms to help keep you balanced. Always look where you are going and not down at your feet! You will hear riders talk about a regular or goofy foot. If you stand with your left foot in front then you are a regular rider, but if your right foot is in front then you're a goofy.

Feel the board

The first trick you must learn is to get used to the feel of moving on a board and wheels! The most important thing is to stay relaxed — this will help your body flex and improve your balance no end. Put your skateboard on a soft surface (lawn or carpet) and try standing on it to get used to its feel. Try different stances until you work out what suits you best. If you need to, ask someone to steady you until you are more confident.

Finding your balance

Skateboarding is all about good balance. Find a flat surface and start off with your front foot on the board. Push slowly with your back foot and get used to the feel of the movement. When you are confident push again and when you are moving lift your back foot onto the deck — now you are skateboarding! Next try some simple crouching movements as you go along. Bend your knees to go slowly down and then up again. Use your arms to keep your balance. This crouching movement is a key move that you will use in many tricks, such as the Ollie (see page 23).

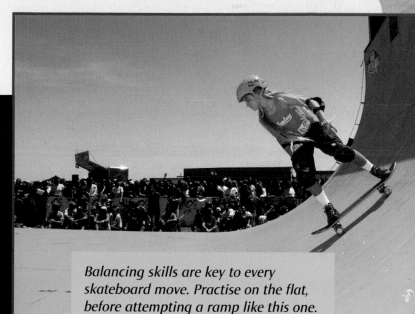

Balancing skills are key to every skateboard move. Practise on the flat, before attempting a ramp like this one.

Falling and bailing

You can't practise tricks without falling. The main thing to remember is to scrunch up and allow yourself to roll, or to use your pads to land. Your board could also become a serious hazard, especially if you land on it. If you feel yourself falling during a trick, bail by kicking your board out of the way.

HOT HINT

Try not to put your hands out when you fall, especially on the vert ramp. It's an automatic reaction, but you are more likely to damage your wrists, hands or even to break an arm. Wear wrist guards to reduce the chance of picking up an injury.

Moving on

When you feel comfortable on your board, it's time to take it up a notch and move on to some key moves and essential tricks. Don't expect to learn these overnight though — even the experts spent many hours learning the basics.

Turning

The trucks and wheels of your skateboard do most of the turning work for you. How quickly you turn will depend on your set-up. Loose-set trucks and small wheels will give sharper turns, but are not as stable. The main thing you have to learn is controlling your weight to start and end a turn. To begin a turn simply shift your weight towards the side of the board you want to turn; your trucks will do the rest. To straighten out shift your weight back again.

Tic tac

This is where you move the nose of your board from side to side by shifting your weight onto the tail of the board so that the nose lifts off the ground. With the nose in the air you can easily pivot your board from side to side. Your front foot controls how high the nose lifts. To come down again simply put your weight back over the nose. The tic tac is good for learning basic weight control.

The Ollie

This is the skateboard jump and the starting point for nearly all skateboard tricks. Popping an Ollie is all about timing and takes a while to master. It is best to learn by watching others, but here are the basics.

* Ride along with your back foot on the tail of the deck (your front foot will be somewhere in the middle) and your knees bent in a crouch position.

* Kick down on the tail to make the board hit the ground and as the front pops up jump with it. As you do so, slide your front foot up the grip tape towards the nose. This will help lift the board and level it out in mid air. Gravity will bring you down again!

* Straighten your legs a little to meet the ground, and then bend them as you touch down to help absorb the impact.

To the limit

Danny Wainwright from the UK popped an Ollie of an amazing 1.13m in February 2000 – the highest ever recorded.

To the limit

The Ollie is named after Alan 'Ollie' Gelfand who invented the most important move in skateboarding back in 1977 when he was just 14 years old.

FROM THE EDGE

'When he [Alan Gelfand] reached the top of the bowl, he used his back foot to horse-kick his tail. This act shot the tail of his board, almost crashing it into the concrete lip. It seemed the harder he kicked it the higher his board would pop or 'Ollie'. I was amazed. I'd never seen anything like that before, and he did it so fast and effortlessly.' Stacy Peralta (left) describing Alan 'Ollie' Gelfand inventing the Ollie in 1977.

Advanced tricks

Most tricks take time to master. They can also be quite risky, so you should not try them until you are ready. It is a good idea to take lessons from someone more experienced. The 50–50 Grind and Kickflip are two popular tricks.

The 50–50 Grind

This is a key street skating move, where you ride your skateboard along an edge, such as a kerb or rail, using the trucks instead of the wheels. You will need to know how to do an Ollie before you try this trick.

✱ Choose what it is you want to grind, and skate alongside it.

✱ When you have picked up some speed (not too fast!) pop an Ollie and aim to land your trucks onto the edge you want to grind.

✱ Bend your legs as you land to absorb the impact and try not to land too heavily, or the board may just stop instead of grinding.

✱ As your board slows and you come to the end of your grind, pop another small Ollie to jump off the object and back to your wheels.

✱ Start with small obstacles, such as a low kerb, and you will soon master the 50–50 Grind. Then you can move on to try other grinds such as the 5–0 Grind (a grind on the rear truck only) and the Nosegrind (using the front truck only).

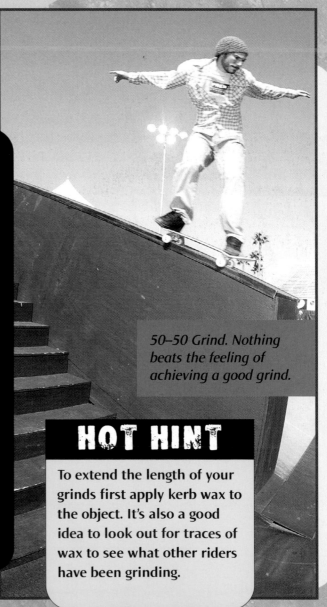

50–50 Grind. Nothing beats the feeling of achieving a good grind.

HOT HINT

To extend the length of your grinds first apply kerb wax to the object. It's also a good idea to look out for traces of wax to see what other riders have been grinding.

To the limit

Curt Lindgren invented the first 'old-school' kickflip in the 1970s, when it was used by freestyle riders as part of their flatland display (tricks performed without ramps). Variations of the old-school kickflip include: the M–80, the 180 Kickflip and the Helicopter.

The Kickflip

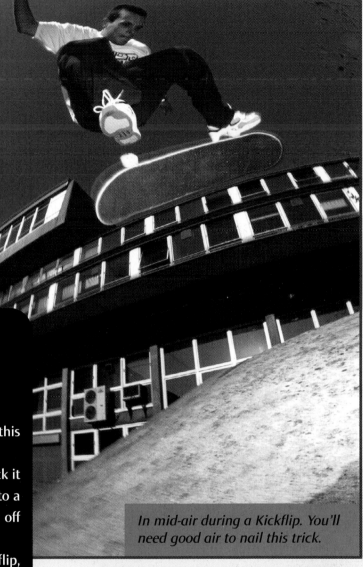

This move was invented by the skating legend Rodney Mullen in 1982, and is an adaption of the old-school kickflip. Mullen's kickflip makes your board flip 360 degrees whilst you are above it in mid-air. To pull a kickflip:

✳ Pop a good Ollie – you will need some height for this so perfect your Ollie first.

✳ As you drag your front foot up the grip tape, flick it off the heel side of your board to set the board into a sideways flip. Make sure you take your back foot off the deck so that it can flip.

✳ Stay above the board and, as it completes the flip, land with your back foot first to stop the board over-flipping.

✳ Remember to flex your knees for a smooth landing and use your arms to help you balance.

In mid-air during a Kickflip. You'll need good air to nail this trick.

HOT HINT

There are instructional DVDs that can show you how to attempt most tricks. Many feature top skateboarding pros, and go through the trick step-by-step. However, the only way to really nail a trick is to keep practising it over and over again.

Get serious!

Most people skateboard for fun, and that's how it should be. If you have lots of ambition and determination, however, then you could take your skateboarding to another level. Here are a few tips that might help you to take your skateboarding to the top.

Practice makes perfect

Don't think that when you have landed a trick once that is it. You will need to keep practising if you want to become the next big name. Even established pros practise for several hours every day – they live and breathe skateboarding. But practice should be fun. If you start to feel sore take a break and come back later.

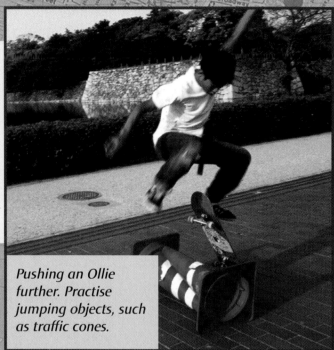

Pushing an Ollie further. Practise jumping objects, such as traffic cones.

Signing autographs during a break. Watching competitions is a great way to learn from others.

Learn from others

Join a skate club, visit skateparks and watch competitions as often as you can. That way you will see others in action, pick up tips and learn new tricks. Most top skaters have learned by skating this way and have then gone on to push themselves further and develop their own style.

Get noticed, get sponsored

All top skaters are sponsored to help them meet the costs of travelling to events and, of course, to keep them kitted out with the latest gear. Many skaters are 'spotted' by sponsors at competitions. This is by far the best way to be seen and if a sponsor thinks you've got what it takes, then they may well offer you a deal. Another way to get noticed is to make your own skate video and send it in to one of the big companies. Be warned though, they are sent hundreds of videos so you'll have to do something special to stand out from the crowd.

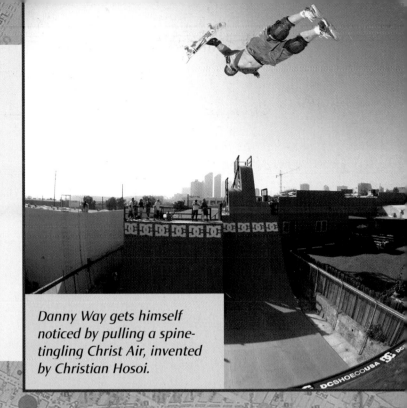

Danny Way gets himself noticed by pulling a spine-tingling Christ Air, invented by Christian Hosoi.

HOT HINT

Get to know the staff at your local skateboard shop. They can be a great source of information about new gear local clubs, competitions and events.

From the left: Buckey Lasek, Sandro Diaz and Bob Burnquest collect their awards.

Go for gold!

To increase your chances of skating stardom you'll have to enter some competitions. Your local skate club or shop will probably have information about competitions happening in your area. Skateboard-scene websites and magazines also regularly feature competition announcements. If you work your way through the competitions, you could one day find yourself going for gold at the X-Games — how else do you think Tony Hawk and Danny Way became skateboarding legends?

FROM THE EDGE

'Being a pro skater would be a dream, but it is a lot of responsibility and commitment. I got into skating because it was fun. If skating was more of a job perhaps I wouldn't enjoy it so much.'
Nick Jensen, street skater, UK

Meet the pros

It is difficult to say who the best skateboarder is because they each have their own style. If you ask around everyone has a personal favourite, but here are some of the seriously big names you can't fail to miss.

Skating legend

The world's most famous (and most successful) skateboarder is Tony Hawk. He began skating when he was just 9 years old in 1977, and by 14 had become a pro. By 16 he was the best skater in the world and dominated the sport for almost two decades. He has entered 103 pro competitions, winning 73 of them and coming second in 19. Tony Hawk retired from competition skating in 1999, but is still active in skating as a promoter and owner of top skateboard company, Birdhouse.

Tony Hawk with a board designed by Birdhouse. He continues to influence the skateboard scene today.

To the limit

Rider profile:

Ryan Sheckler or 'Fly'n Ryan' was just 13 years old when he won gold in the X-Games Park event — the youngest X-Games winner ever. He went on to win nearly every major street event in 2003 and became the world's number one street skater. Unfortunately, Ryan failed to pick up a medal at the 2004 X-Games.

To the limit

Rider profile:

Paul Rodriguez or 'P-Rod' turned pro at 17 in 2002 and in 2003 rode off with bronze in his first X-Games Street event. He lost out that year to his hero and gold medallist Eric Koston who, with four other X-Games medals, is one of skating's biggest names.

FROM THE EDGE

'Every kid that skates, that's their dream [to turn pro]. When your dream finally comes true, it's pretty tight. I remember when I was younger, for me and all my friends, our goal was to be pro. I'm not the kid looking up to the guys anymore. I feel like I'm in the cool club or something.' Paul 'P-Rod' Rodriguez discusses going pro

Catching up fast

Most pro skateboarders are men, but girls and women like to skate too and are catching up fast. Cara-Beth Burnside ('CB') was one of the first professional women skaters and has competed in men's competitions since 1991. She helped put women's skateboarding on the map. Other key women in skateboarding include Amy Caron, Lauren Perkins and Elissa Steamer who won the women's X-Games Street event in 2004.

FROM THE EDGE

'It's nice to have a handful of girls out there who are charging and learning new tricks, it's motivating for me; I like being around that. It hasn't been around for very long.'
Cara-Beth Burnside (right)

Jargon buster

air — riding with all four wheels off the ground; short for aerial.

backside — when a trick or turn is executed with the skater's back facing the ramp or obstacle.

concussion — a severe blow to the head that often results in a loss of consciousness.

deck — the flat standing surface of a skateboard, usually laminated maple.

dropping-in — skateboarding down off the top of a ramp platform.

Frontside — when a trick or turn is executed with the front of the skater's body facing the ramp or obstacle.

goofy foot — riding with the right foot forward, the opposite of 'regular foot'.

grind — scraping one or both trucks on a kerb, railing, or other surface.

grip tape — a gritty layer stuck to the top of the deck to help a rider's shoes grip the board.

halfpipe — a U-shaped ramp of any size, usually with a flat section at the bottom.

jam — an informal event or gathering of skateboarders at a skatepark or similar location.

Kickflip — a variation on the Ollie in which the skater kicks the board into a spin before landing back on it.

nail — to successfully complete a trick.

Ollie — a jump performed by tapping the tail of the board on the ground; the basis of most skating tricks.

rail — the edge of the skateboard, also, a handrail used for railslides.

railslide — a trick in which the skater slides the base of the deck along a rail.

regular Foot — riding with the left foot forward, the opposite of 'goofy foot'.

Street skating — skating on streets, kerbs, benches, handrails and other elements of street furniture.

trucks — the front and rear axle assemblies that connect the wheels to the deck and provide the turning capabilities for the board.

vert ramp — a halfpipe, usually at least 2.5 metres tall, with steep sides that are perfectly vertical near the top. There are now super ramps and mega ramps.

Vert skating — skating on ramps and other vertical structures specifically designed for skating.

Find out more

Every effort has been made by the Publishers to ensure that these websites contain no inappropriate or offensive material. However, because of the nature of the Internet, it is impossible to guarantee that the contents of these sites will not be altered. We strongly advise that Internet access is supervised by a responsible adult.

www.lushlongboards.com

A UK site offering everything to do with longboarding. It also has information on mountain boarding and an online skate school for useful tips.

www.allgirlskatejam.com

Website of the AGSJ, established by Patty Segovia to promote female skateboarders. Features event coverage and an image gallery.

www.radlands.com

Radlands in Northampton, England is one of the world's ultimate skateparks. Find out about upcoming events or find out how to plan a session there yourself.

www.boarding.com/skate/index.html

Latest news, competition results and useful tips. There is even a section that tells you how to build you own vert ramp.

www.spausa.org

The Skate Park Association of the United States of America (SPAUSA). Find out all about skateparks in the home of skateboarding.

www.skateboarding.com

The website of Transworld Skateboarding features online trick videos, live coverage of skateboarding events and product reviews.

www.slalomskateboarder.com

For all you want to know about slalom skateboarding, including news, gear reviews and the latest competition information.

www.bobstricktips.com/

This is a great site to learn all those skateboarding tricks from the basic 'Ollie' through to the '360 Nose Shove It'! All tricks have photos and video clips to help you perfect them.

www.dannyway.com

The official Danny Way website. Find out about this crazy world record breaking skater. Make sure you check out the mega ramp section with amazing video clips.

ww.nzskateboarding.com

The home of skateboarding in New Zealand, this website features interviews, the latest news, trick tips and images.

Index